Poems and Micropoems

by
Ram Krishna Singh

Poems and Micropoems

by Ram Krishna Singh

Poems and Micropoems

By Ram Krishna Singh

First Edition

Content Copyright © 2023 by Ram Krishna Singh

Author: Ram Krishna Singh
Editor: Paul Gilliland
Formatting: Southern Arizona Press
Cover Artwork: Linnaea Mallette

Published by Southern Arizona Press
Sierra Vista, Arizona 85635
www.SouthernArizonaPress.com

ISBN: 978-1-960038-08-1

Poetry

Acknowledgements

The volume contains some of my poems and micropoems composed during the last two years. Most of the micropoems are in the nature of haiku and tanka which continue to happen, and some of these have appeared in both online and print journals or popular social media such as Facebook and Twitter.

Grateful acknowledgement is made to the editors and publishers of the following journals and anthologies that first used some of the poems, including haiku and tanka, collected here:

Poetcrit, Creative Flight Journal, Writers Editors Critics, Scarlet Dragonfly Journal, The United Haiku and Tanka Society Anthology: Songbirds Online 2022, Madness: An Anthology of World Poetry, SHE, Better Than Starbucks, Minuto de Poesia, Lothlorien Poetry Journal, VSANA, and Haiku Universe.

I am indebted to Southern Arizona Press for their support to my creativity and publishing this collection of poems.

-R.K.Singh

Contents

Poems

Micropoems

Poems

Nature is Me

Nature is me
seeking my place
in the star through births

now memory
wild maze of conceit
and darkness

yet a tiny part
a dew drop
dotted with beauty

The Hell is Real

They lure me with wealth in heaven
as if plucking hair would reduce
weight of the dead body

they don't see the bruises abandoned
on the fading skin of apple
that rolls metaphors in the basket

sleeplessly I watch her drift in dreams
on the horizon float to descend
for a share in the horrors of earth

they blindly conceal to hoodwink
god's will for poets cultured in the past
now glittering as the sun's wreckage

I can't clean nor rebuild around them
the hell is real I can't run away
with sweet nothings   I can't die in bluffs

Here and Now

I don't deify poets or politicians
nor trade in faith for bread

I don't sell gods and goddesses
spirit is not my profession

nor do I give moral discourse
for life in the next world

I am a man like millions
who dream   struggle and die

and nobody mourns
my drifty silence

hidden in darkness
flecks of light

enough to weigh down
here and now

Cry of a Mother

Why do they ignore the clitoris when half the world has it?
the lovers don't care   the doctors don't talk

it's no leaf that falls on the wave's crest
and rots on the shore before they prescribe
a chocolate remedy or testosterone cream
to revive in dapple light:

denial is the way of life
be it desire emotion or frailty
for conformity unity and control

the redness of the setting or rising sun
is too much to the drab colours of the priests
who accuse of heresy witchcraft or immorality
to shut the so-called hotbeds of sedition

when all they seek is stoppage
of the show of teeth blood and skull
in the spinning wheel
condemned to nursing home

Love by Default

When you deny love lies in fucking you cheat
millions of starving lovers smelling sex
in each encounter or dating a woman
whose hunger is different each time she meets man

to say the unsaid or live the fleeing joy
or weep longingly   recall the days gone by
or rue only if it were as it once was

lying on his back like whales he lets the ships pass
and clasps a drowning one as he gasps for air
and she yields her body to love by default

Locked

Eagle's shadow
on the still boat on bank
blank page of tomb
that sank without history
of women who anchored
life now locked within
sandy rocks disguising faith
in phallic images
drunken politics
of carving and curving
on the potter's wheel

On the Edge

She rises from stone gate
with searching eyes
for passion flower
stays for a while and goes
making promise of return
to sleep with me once
before the last good bye

New Slavery

From the 15th floor window I watch
dreams racing on the muddied road
the ugly beauty of tomorrow

the romance of the miserable
the egotist the cunning the heart-broken
the idealist the maniacs the enlightened cheats

the crafty and the unlucky too
who conceal cavity in their shoes
in the gallery of Great Tech Game

fabricating newer lies and hypocrisies
of saffron politics secular faith and people's power
spilling blood to heal history of wrongs

create new cultural fantasy
new racism   new slavery
home grown narcissistic lords and ladies

Narcissist

Seventy-five years
no development
he brags to self-brand
democracy of
divide and disturb
peace with rhetoric
woos with fabrications
like Trump deludes histories
adds novel culture
to keep his hands clean

Curse

PM Modi reminds
River Ganga called him
to do all that she wants

he builds for Banares
altars and corridor
by the riverside

people see the wilderness
the bones of enemies:
cursed is he who curses him

with eyes wide open
he sees vision of Shiva
and pushes me back

Disguise

Myths devour
life now in symbols
mortar and brick
pillars and lies disguise
cycles of truth and search

to feel good
they look back and riot:
Gyanvapi
don't see Jerusalem
timeless strife of history

Ukraine War

Enchained by his own
creation in Ukraine
Zilensky now counts

his own wounds and sees
a spectacle of ravage
before extinction

Joe Biden couldn't help
the avalanche of night
now wrapped in rubble

none left to shed tears
keep memories of the sun
now steeped in darkness

Aid

Mid-October
each day afternoon rains
no expiry date
potholes keep growing large
houses keep collapsing

and here they are
minting money in bids
for gravel and cure
from flood and cyclone raging
with politics of aid

Parody

Is nationalism Hindutva
or right reactionaryism
for political security
of the likes of Modis, Xis, Putins
that play games of disorder
with a Biden and dictate
new rhetoric of regression and repression
at home the hope and hysteria
is dying and no Ayodhya
Mathura or Gyanvapi can win
votes of loyals and traitors
without mutual right to exist
without obscurantism and reform
parody of promises

It Doesn't Happen Here Alone

In the Congress
a Republican law maker*
condemns same-sex
marriage three days ago
now attends wedding of
his gay son with
the love of his life   reports
Centre Daily
in defence he questions
the Democrats' silence
about nuptial
of historic inflation
and price rise at
petrol pumps and grocery stores

*[*United States Representative Glenn Thomson, reported on nbcnews.com
on 26 July 2022]*

Wellness

It's no paradise
but sounds filter upwards
from small Smondo shops
live-in couples in Neotown
share thrills of touch and hug
older couples miss
while walking or watching
alone from windows
gauge their depth of feelings
and monetary wellness

Cry for Alternative

There is a whole lot of crowded life under the long flyover
--from fish market to plastic tents and car parking to
excretion—
poor pedestrians can't cross the road either side

they fear auto rickshaws   bikes food stalls pushes and
pickpockets
on the footpath extended shops short-circuit every movement
opposite Paras Cancer Centre in Raja Bazar

it's a sight of sepsis with multiple dysfunction
--a consilience of rural ambition with urban abundance—
they cry for alternative diagnosis but lack doctor and ventilator

None Would Fix

I couldn't blame anyone
I just kept praying

it was hot soup
it burnt my lips

I couldn't be still
I couldn't wait

it was money
the bank didn't credit

it was tax
they had bungled

I couldn't be patient
I couldn't sleep

called an expert
in human dishonesty

cursed manipulation
of systemic truth

they suffer   we suffer
but none would fix

Just in Case…

With structural corruption
embedded in system
who can change
the future course:

in their stinking nests
the owls and rats plan for
booster shots, just in case…

dooms day is a long dream

the pandemic cements
differences for eon

standing before a narrow spine
the dead claim the summit
without reaching the top

I don't know how to set down
my burden and move ahead

Azaan

Precarious
at the threshold of sleep
the *azaan*
only a deprived
muezzin knows

behind the mosque
the peepal guards
mafia mansion
in lantern light
god's business

Temple

Known a man of his word
before exiting the windowless hall
scrawls his bearded sinisterity
none could read: he proves a rhino
turning the temple into funeral home

Whispers

The sim flame beneath my tea
the birds perching on branches
I hear the chill whispers
between the leaves
shadows rustle with wind
the world rolls on its own pace

Nobody Asks Me

From lattice window
I watch the doomed and dying each day

read the tattooed name
of her first love on the right arm

waking up the drunk
with tenderness of youthful mom

bitchy fight at night
for booze or sex in candle light

smoking dreams of years
with dirt or grease between fingers

his somniloquy
drugged-out face   doomed grin   boys' dustup

now the covid smells
they shift lamp to live with shadow

lockdown images
burning   buried   floating bodies

I nearly die everyday
nobody asks me my last wish

Routine

School buses blow horn
one after other at gate
parents rush with bags
bottles and reluctant kids
each morning the same routine

before they proceed
to work station with laptop
tension of meeting
fear of takeover   bank loan
and night's bitterness in bed

Dog Days

A numerologist says
I was born to attract abundance
and draws a cosmic soul reading
when a breakthrough is due

and here I am ruing my dog days

will I get the pension
before the wealth planet expires
from my home to others?

I can't buy magic pendant
for Venus to level up my life
or make real the dream numbers

Love

Rocking chair:
sun through the clouds in
verandah
after days of rain
and nostalgic nights

she hands me
a lukewarm tea of
ginger clove
and honey to make
love and stay alive

Leaks

Cobwebs in the mind
breed smelly thoughts
years couldn't erase:

life leaks hanging on
the condom tit
between two bangers

Smile

Shadows fly from my fingers
with the moving wrist—
the hand disappears

I can't touch her heart
under the tan skin:
they waver behind the glass

hissing through clenched teeth
as I sip my drink
she gives me a frozen smile

Victim

She's graceful
on bended knees
supplicant
head bent   in peace

victim of whip
can't pull back
past happiness
love's sharp tongue

he's no lug
can't see the gems
in rain drops
her aura shines

Meditation

Miles away
stars cease to twinkle
no new moon

smell sound air or life
a new loneliness
shrouds earthy sadness

in mind's cave
wrinkled eyelids couch
returning light

Boredom

Do I not deceive myself
in the unending flux of time?

too worried about the future
only suffer the present
or kill it for the sin of bread?

now post the covers of my books
on my timeline and renew
the past I never enjoyed

they think I live blissfully
in the locked hive of academics

Rights

Mist in the eyes
holes in the soles
and no plan-B
to hit Goliath

who cares I'm a poet
without day job
or pension for food
and medicines to live?

I too have rights
but I'm no politician
or seer with cheat code
to tame shadows

One More Poem Born

I don't long for the past that swings and rings
I don't care for the future I colour
with empty wishes prayers and meditation

dreams' dark inspiration carves the present
I suffer more at night than in the day
breathe hell seeking freedom in the body

through friends in spirit turn sanguine despite
the tricky degeneration in shared life
one more day passes   one more poem born

Nemesis

Climate crisis:
light bulb in the head goes off
where's green future?

weekly depression with mask
in dying park breathe fake news
panoramic nuisance

in shrinking space gowks
guck with sliming lips
nature's nemesis

Lies

In life's open book
they all have a lie or two
concealed for truths

to reveal tranquil
conscience unstung by snake
sleeping deep in heart

Micropoems

Haiku

new moon
rocking her world—
twin flames

***

verandah—
touching her naked skin
morning breeze

***

seashore—
waves rush to squeeze
feet in sand

***

flour dough
between the fingers
despair sticks

***

her hair up
transparent front and back:
birthday cake

***

her soul touch
vibrating the depth
in darkness

midnight moon
senses aroused—
lift the veil

***

sex excels a host of sins love hides

***

yawning yet waiting for making love

***

pecking behind the mask magic-seekers

***

watching rhythm of ripples in fish pond at home

***

too beautiful to catch
the girl and butterfly

***

diving deep a swimmer
in the stream of time

***

clicking jaw and cracking knees
I touch the sounds of ageing

a politician
is a crook
with silence
sthitprajna

***

her soft throat
raises high to sacred space
than prayer

***

each winter
different from the gone one:
virus variant

***

left alone
a covid patient
restlessly turns

***

breathless
search for airy room
underground

***

without silver wings
she hugs angels in the blue
becomes a star

mid-June morning—
the gardener's muddy fingers
scratch the itching scalp

***

one with granite tub
a beetle in the bathroom—
silence of dampness

***

threatening rain
dark clouds hang over still trees—
smelly clothesline

***

shortening shadow
of the window in my room—
time to wind up work

***

creepy shadows
along the muddy road—
big bright moon

***

raining night--
she shuts the window
saves his books

silence—
her eyes word
wine song

***

high minaret
recorded call for namaaz
soul's melody

***

in the wild
inner echoes—
dragonfly

***

giant wind—
sail through the cavity
in the tide

***

chaos in sky
dark with colour and light
waves on beach

***

red with shame
the sky at sunrise
one more kiss

they watch from the street
our embrace at the window
sneak into liquor

***

a sweating couple
sip iced coffee in beer mugs—
highway *dhaaba*

***

hands sweaty
heart pounding:
secret message

***

thrice she clicks
her heels together:
secret code

***

her sharp nail draws
love sign on the stone's back--
green patina

***

nude statues
pursuit of pleasure—
sex tourism

stone stairs on the ghat
childhood nostalgia—
dog days of August

***

melts under the feet
grey sadness of sand on the shore—
blue waves in stone

***

on the roadside
zero-figure women
waiting for bus

***

too complex
the calculus of grief:
forgotten fractals

***

inauspicious
this morning my tooth cracks:
winter solstice

***

I turn on room heater
it doesn't heat—
solstice evening

shadowy hope
vanishing teeth and hair—
73rd birthday

***

distanced from sun
in A C cabin
low level Vit. D

***

awake with
neighbour's weeping dog—
more death news

***

absent spirit
planetary transit:
halcyon years

***

tarot prophet:
taking last order for
heart cleanser

***

the fire blazes up
from body to mind to speech
heat is what we eat

the end of dream is sleep
the mind and senses rest
the breath stays awake

***

past lover
time to clean up house:
cold moon

***

in 22
missing life to live alive:
frozen courage

***

half of my mind on God
and the other half on sex:
eternal hunger

***

how could he stop
in the middle of sex
to eat kebab?

***

wearing wishes
for money miracles—
green adamite

searching truth
a homeless wanderer—
shoreless sea

***

rioting flames
witches dance in cave—
strawberry moon

***

sunny morning
no kites flying in the sky:
Makar Sankranti

***

smoggy day:
can't remember when
life was good

***

shattered self--
lost the light in silent scream
of darkness

***

still new
last year's mask:
Halloween

a fleeting shadow
on the kitchen wall—
one more sun

***

love in folds of sleep
forgotten memories:
washed up melody

***

how sweet the juice
of trees and flowers bees make—
honey is one

***

looking for light
hidden in darkness
drifty silence

***

old diary—
finding phone numbers
of friends still alive

***

dark fears—
loping in the street
mantra on lips

lonely hours
restlessness of night
breathe satyr

***

love touch
spirit's spring time:
new day

***

she says she's single
and ready to mingle
just moments away

***

awake, cross-legged
till witching hour—
no means no

***

smelling
turkey left-overs—
thanksgiving

***

post cyclone
stagnant water in field—
fishing drought

fanaticism
preached with herbs and spices—
broken health line

***

the year ends
let's go fly a kite—
sunny day

***

people trust
what utopia looks like:
lighted banks of Saryu

***

intangible
psychic insights:
moments of muck

***

holiday season:
she takes a deep breath
looks at the map

***

on his epitaph:
he died protesting land tax
on his grave

Tanka

can't tackle big beasts
and the sheeple that snigger
candle procession:
read silent tears on the cheeks
of the mother of the lynched

***

dining table
resting place for the dust
my mind emits
before her third eye opens
I switch on the AC

***

a one-eyed woman
the window curtain shakes
nightly stillness
veronal dread in hell
breeches itch in half-sleep

***

the musky sillage
confirms her presence nearby
in cold sun I wait
for beer with her one last time
get drowned in her wild kisses

her lips
crimson with *paan*
stings my heart:
smell of saffron and cardamom
melts in my haiku

***

dream-incited
I awake with a start
to her promise
sleeping together once
more before we depart

***

grey morning
shivering body
walk back home
to the drizzling din
of a muddied street

***

lightning—
roaring colours in the sky
red white dark
merge into one
fire water earth

late night—
not many drink
at home
wait for the end
the bed sinks the body

***

what poem can brew
on faces hidden behind
veils misty eyes say
all I can't image in
haiku with season word

***

Manikarnika:
he collects warm ashes
searching gold to live
by country liquor or bread
for starving wife or children

***

wailing over
adversaries that seek good
and do evil
he asks how long the dead
be denied condemnation

to own her body
they look for slave market—
civilized rapists
with empty pocket force sun
light into nocturnal bed

***

wintered sadness
different dimensions—
nature's cycle
unable to cope
zen meditation

***

down the roof gutter
rain water gurgle too loud
she shouts at neighbours
disturbing peace and sleep
blaming rural culture

***

they publish rubbish but
seek bone-deep art that whips
the ass housed in metro
when winter comes shut the door
complaining rancid taste

from head to heel
feel coldness of the floor:
summer morning
shavasan in AC
refreshing veronal

***

each syllable
allergic pollen and dust
her autumn tongue
one more song to prick with
new variant, new wound

***

the nagging pains
in the index finger joints
kills all poetry
of body and mind at night
I yell sighs in half-sleep

***

winter arrives with
wheezing sneezing and backache
whole night without sleep
I try pills to get better
lamenting ageing and pray

no temple
this body degenerates
memory fades
stinking remains
can't forget all

***

naked in debris
a crying baby girl
he bends to pick up
eyes wander to locate
her mother too nearby

***

thoughtless mind
weeds and refuse buried
empty heart
illusion of self thrown out
yet the guest doesn't visit

***

seeing the body
in her lingerie drying
on clothesline
and pretend reading
the morning news

an old lady
calling heart-centred men
to awaken
in three sessions their full
potential in bed and beyond

***

her beauty
smells the soil that sings
grace in look:
I whisper my heart and chase
the glow her shadow spreads

***

she draws a church
on the back of a leaflet
to resurrect Mary
in whose name she cried for years
and none counted her tears

***

sitting by the road
she plays the harlot for bread
men sin, she suffers
from police raid to VD
they gift with morbid morals

young and married
her body a burden
can't help herself
reduced to a donkey
suffering morality

***

seashore:
she lies on her back
eyes closed
feels foam on the waves
butterflies too

***

his son views letters
on the billboard a sparrow
awaits green light
for the road to be free
to peck at the fallen grains

***

unpredictable
monsoon clouds in Bangalore
confusion all time:
wet again my walking shoes
mud splashes by running car

morning walk:
two boys going to school
pick plump jamuns
rolling on the roadside
for tiffin at recess

***

puff by puff
smoke away their tension
trainee programmers
on the roadside mixed smell
of sweat and talcum powder

***

a walking woman
pregnant from the back raising
hand for her man's hand
a little away holding
the cell phone to his ear

***

an old woman
steals hibiscus from our gate
grinning *nav-ratri*
puja at home and hurries
back before my wife confronts

from Shiva's temple
high decibel puja noise
wrath of the goddess
she prays for long power cut
for her short meditation

***

sham of puja
ruddy garland round the neck
kneel to quench the thirst
with rum and goat meat invoke
the goddess for sex at night

***

share memories
in the dark of night—
race for life
brave scents from the brink
mate kisses with grace

***

every home
Shiva's monastery:
cannabis
no secrets or lies
relish special tea

giving to grow
intimacy:
wants no trouble
realizing dream life
on daily basis

***

anti-national
every dissenting voice—
lotus regime
bullying the generation
with changing narratives

***

no firsts in hunger:
they all push one another
for a pail of rice
to cook without fire, roof and
utensils lost in landslide

***

a sleeping man
under the tree
awaits a grave
villains in village keep
gaslighting all day

Poems and Micropoems

About the Author

Ram Krishna Singh, also known as R.K. Singh, has been writing for over four decades. Born (31 December 1950), brought up and educated in Varanasi, he has been professionally concerned with teaching and research in the areas of English language teaching, especially for Science and Technology, and Indian English Poetry practices. Till the end of 2015, Professor of English at IIT-ISM in Dhanbad, Dr Singh has published 52 books, including poetry collections *God Too Awaits Light* (2017), *Growing Within / Desăvârşire lăuntrică* (English / Romanian, 2017), *There's No Paradise and Other Selected Poems Tanka & Haiku* (2019), *Tainted With Prayers / Contaminado con oraciones* (English / Spanish, 2019), *Silencio: Blanca desconfianza: Silence: White distrust* (Spanish edition, Kindle, Spanish / English, 2021), *A Lone Sparrow* (English / Arabic, 2021), *Against the Waves: Selected Poems* (2021), *Changing Seasons: Selected Tanka and Haiku* (English / Arabic, 2021), *Covid-19 And Surge of Silence / Kovid-19 Hem Sessízlík Tolkînî* (English / Tatar, 2021), and 濁: SILENCE: A WHITE DISTRUST (English / Japanese, Kindle Edition/Paperback, 2022). His haiku and tanka have been internationally read, appreciated and translated into several languages, including French, Spanish, Romanian, Chinese, Serbian, Croatian, Slovene, Bosnian, Hungarian, Albanian, Irish, Japanese, Bulgarian, Russian, German, Italian, Portuguese, Greek, Crimean Tatar, Arabic, Farsi, and Hindi. His awards and honors include Ritsumeikan University Peace Museum Award, Kyoto, 1999, Certificate of Honor and Nyuusen Prize, Kumamoto, 2000 and 2008, Lifetime Achievement Award of the International Poets Academy, Chennai, 2009, Prize of Corea Literature, South Korea, 2013, Aichi Prefecture Board of Education Award, Japan, 2015, Naji Naaman's Literary Prize, Lebanon, 2015, nomination for Pushcart Prize, 2013, 2014, and Citation of Brightest Honour, International Sufi Centre: Sufi World, Bangalore, September 2020.

Follow him at:
https://pennyspoetry.wikia.com/wiki/R.K._Singh.

email: profrksingh@gmail.com.

Additional Works

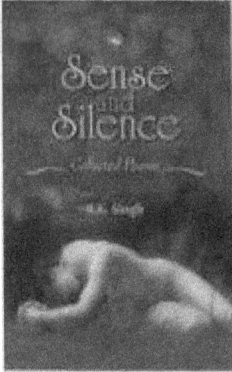

Sense and Silence
(Jaipur: Vyking Books, 2010)

https://www.amazon.in/Sense-Silence-
Collected-Poems-Singh/dp/8191058820

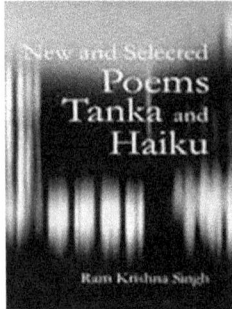

New and Selected Poems: Tanka and Haiku
(New Delhi: Authors Press, 2012)

https://www.amazon.in/New-Selected-Poems-
Tanka-Haiku/dp/8172736355

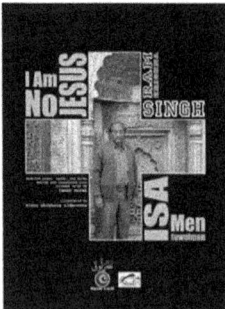

**I Am No Jesus: and other selected Poems,
tanka, and haiku**
(Iaşi: Editura StudIS, 2014)

https://www.amazon.com/Am-No-Jesus-other-
selected/dp/6066245627

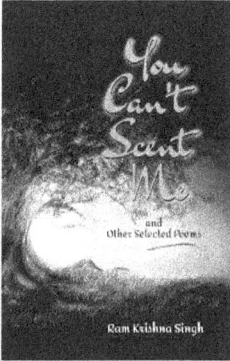

You Can't Scent Me and Other Selected Poems
(New Delhi: Authors Press, 2016)

https://www.amazon.in/cant-Scent-Other-Selected-Poems/dp/9352072634

God Too Awaits Light
(Joshua Tree, California: Cholla Needles, 2017)

https://www.amazon.com/God-Awaits-Light-Krishna-Singh/dp/1975993845

Growing Within/Desăvârşire lăuntrică
(English/Romanian, Constanta: Anticus Press, 2017)

https://issuu.com/anticusmulticultural/docs/growing_within_online

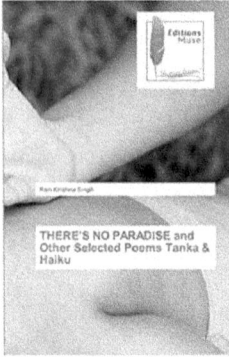

There's No Paradise and Other Selected Poems
(French Edition. Editions Muse, 2019)

https://www.amazon.ae/THERES-PARADISE-
Other-Selected-Poems/dp/6202292474

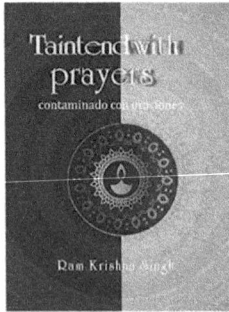

Tainted with Prayers: Contaminado con
Oraciones
(Colombia: Editorial Ave Viajera SAS, 2020)

https://www.amazon.com/Tainted-Prayers-Ram-
Krishna-Singh/dp/1650109237

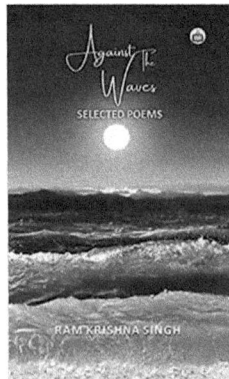

Against the Waves: Selected Poems
(New Delhi: Authors Press, 2021)

https://www.amazon.in/Against-Waves-Ram-
Krishna-Singh/dp/B0953RT4Y1

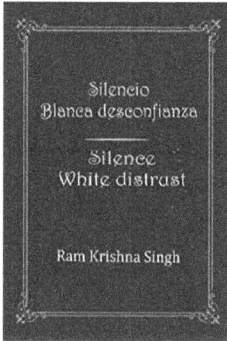

Silencio: Blanca Desconfianza: Silence: White Distrust
(Spanish Edition, Spanish/English, Kindle, 2021)

https://www.amazon.com/Silencio-desconfianza-Silence-distrust-Spanish-ebook/dp/B08XWHTG19

白濁 : *Silence: A White Distrust*
(Japanese edition. Tr. Rika Inami. Kindle/Paperback, 2022)

https://www.amazon.ae/%E7%99%BD%E6%BF%81-SILENCE-DISTRUST-%E7%A8%B2%E7%BE%8E-%E9%87%8C%E4%BD%B3/dp/B09RG5CZB2

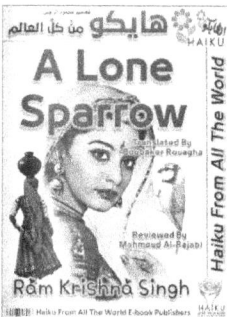

A Lone Sparrow
(e-book. English/Arabic. calameo.com, 2021)

https://en.calameo.com/books/0035528310acd5f93da63

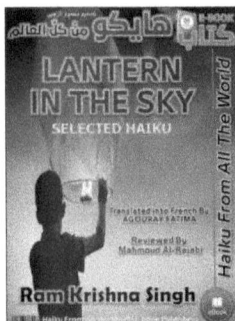

Lantern in the Sky: Selected Haiku
(e-book.English/French. calameo.com, 2022)

https://en.calameo.com/books/00355283109dc8
0c7b0db

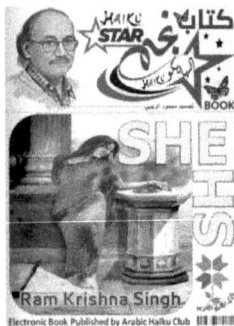

SHE
(e-book. English. Arabic Haiku Club, 2022)

https://en.calameo.com/books/00355283198a95
0fde5f8

Drifty Silence
(e-book. English. Arabic Haiku Club, 2023)

https://en.calameo.com/books/0035528318f144
6b803f1

www.ingramcontent.com/pod-product-compliance
Lightning Source LLC
Chambersburg PA
CBHW071841020426
42331CB00007B/1819